For the Animals

Poems
by

LJ Ireton

(Second Edition)

For all the animal charities

*(Especially The Humane League UK,
Viva!, Humane Society International
and Cats Protection)*

Thanks to:

Amazon/Kindle publishing

My husband and my two rescue cats.

The animals I have met who inspire me.

The Humane League UK for supporting my poetry.

Contents

1-5.	Acknowledgements
6-7.	Contents
8.	Animal Shelter
9.	Hatchlings
10.	Ghost
11-12.	Milk
13.	Listening
14.	Life
15-16.	Animals Around
17-18.	Animals Haiku
19-20.	Solace
21.	The World is a Cat
22.	Crazy Cat Lady
23.	An old man and his dog
24-25.	Beings
26-27.	Species
28.	Watching
29.	My Ark
30.	Eden
31.	Animals Haiku
32.	Dairy
33-34.	For the Animals
35.	Rescue Haiku
36.	Animals Haiku
37.	Elsewhere

38-39.   Seen
40.   Attention
41-43.   About LJ
44-45.   Find out more

Animal Shelter

I know the Wild
Has its own Way –
A prowling life
Of predators, prey.

But here the wolves
Wear a human face
And hunting is
An amusement game.

So I'll protect you
While I can –
Not from animals,
But from man.

Hatchlings

They do no wrong.
They hatch, they cheep
And start to look around
At scattered egg shells
And matching eyes, set
In hatchling soft, soft, down
That we replicate as fluffy toys
And put their image on sale
As they are killed and thrown as trash
Because they were born male.

Ghost

What have humans done?
That even animals can't be
Animals
When they're your own creation
Or rather
Alteration
Your food has a face
And it's as white as a ghost
You took its colours away
For your gain.

Milk

Get up, little one
I've licked you clean
You can stand now
Stand by me.

Your eyes are mine
My milk is yours
Take shelter
Under me.

I call to you
Because the men
They take you
Stay with me.

And on my own
All I know then
Is the space where
You should be.

Listening

Listening to an animal
Engages the heart
In imagination,
Moving the mind to find
A compassion
Lost in humans
Long ago.

Life

If we saw life as children do,
Light would let the spectrum through
We'd find surprise in tiny things –
Flower petals or fairy wings?
Sand would become sparkle dust,
Forest dwellings wanderlust.
We'd seek the unicorns in the trees
And feel their magic in the breeze –
See all the animals as miracles too,
Offer them tea cups, as children do.

Animals Around

I don't feel at home
Without animals around.
The sea and the sky
Need the birds to cry
Over the waves to fly
Across the Sun
To complete the sound.

I don't feel at home
Without animals around.
There is no Eden now,
But maybe God gifts
Us animals
As a souvenir
Of sacred ground.

I am only sane
In a room of animals –
Humans confuse me.

Solace

I sought solace with swans
After too much human noise
Their shapes on sunlit water
Soothed an ache inside my mind.

A person, then another
Held out hands to feed a swan
But held no food, just photo smiles -
The bird's expectations undone.

And just like that, the camera flash
Burnt my bubbling peace
Humans tricked the birds
So now, again, they troubled me.

The World is a Cat

The world is a cat –
Her belly, the ocean
The land marks her back
A forest in motion
The waves of the moon
Are found in her eyes
The stripes of the tree trunks
Run down her side.
In one perfect jump,
Fierce and softness collide
Yes, the world is a cat –
Fire and water, combined.

Crazy Cat Lady

Crazy cat lady
Feeding the felines
While wearing weird clothes
And talking back to them
And always about them
All the cats
'She doesn't need any more!'

I think she's beautiful
Her gift is giving
And her cloak is compassion
She listens to creatures
While others ignore them
All that love
The world needs more.

An old man and his dog

An old man and his dog
Sauntered slowly up to me
He pointed at the bird picture
I'd wanted him to see
Then pointed back down at his dog,
Said "He's just like him, like me"
And I thought as he walked away
Yes, that's it completely.

Beings

They're frightened.
Little hearts beat in alarm
Little lives form a death drum –
One after one after one
They drop off the spectrum
Of beings who feel
Because humans don't feel
It's a problem.
So the animals fear,
Understand,
While humans become numb.

Species

In your eyes
I see all eyes
Held in different shapes
Who feel the same
As you do
Destined for other fates
For what reason?
There is no reason
To distinguish heart from heart
To share a home
With one
Should pardon
The whole
And not the part.

Watching

Watching
Sea creatures
Of the deep on TV
In awe of their complexity
They build a community
These tiny fish
Coloured with intellect
Yet humanity's disconnect
Puts them on plates
Eating
The stills of reality.

My Ark

There need be no flood,
No water around
For me to build my ark.
There is danger enough
On the expanse of our ground
For me to make a start.
No spears, no knives, no guns
No greed
Will come aboard this ship.
All kinds of kind
Will sit inside
While man's cruel reign still drips.

Eden

Eden eyes don't separate
The species into types
That we can eat or
We can keep –
They see the souls inside.

Eden ears appreciate
The sounds of all who talk
Like speaks to like, but
Love speaks to be kind
In any language or birdsong.

Eden minds affiliate
The leopard with the lamb –
Herd and pride
Sit side by side –
Animal and man.

Labels and pictures
Lie about the animals
Truth is meeting them

Dairy

What makes humans do these things
to cows to get their milk?
Some say dairy's ok because at least
There's no blood spilt -
But impregnation by a hand is
not the way of the earth
To feed humans their babies' milk
Is not why cows give birth
Naturally no newborn should be
taken from its mother,
Tube forced down its throat and its milk
given to another
Us! Who do not need it
Cause a mother cow to cry
I don't know how society
Has made this normalized.

For the Animals

Every green plant
For every red heart –
The way the Earth started
For the animals.

But human greed grew
And from their own, drew
Life as new food
From the animals.

Now there is discord –
Creatures great and small
Get what man lets fall
For the animals.

They wait by the doors
You can turn their life around
But they will change yours

Animals seek the
Warmth of your heart, be careful
With theirs in your hands

Elsewhere

I sit in
Silence
But I'm always aware
Of the sound of suffering
Elsewhere
I feel useless
I pray for us to
Show kindness
To the
Smallest
In our care.

38

Seen

For you who suffer behind walls
We will be your windows
On bricks we'll hold up squares of you
Reflections from the shadows
Outside, outside demands you, yet
Outside you'll never see
We will face outside for you
Your faces will be seen.

(Dedicated to *The Humane League UK*)

Attention

Foot after foot and ten thousand arms
Unison shouts, sounding drums and alarms
We need to do this, to stand up for truth
But people are looking at us and not
You.

LJ Ireton has a 1st Class BA Honours in English Literature and Language from The University of Liverpool and works in publishing.

Her first collection of poetry: *Wild Heart* was self-published worldwide on Amazon in July 2017. Her collection of animal poems: *Animal Shelter* was featured in *The Cat* Magazine summer 2018 issue.

As a songwriter, she has had five top 40 musical EPs on iTunes and featured on a number 1 iTunes dance album in the US.

She is a vegan who is passionate about animal rights and welfare. She volunteers at an animal rescue shelter and with a vegan charity in her free time as an advocate and activist.

More poetry collections from LJ Ireton:

Wild Heart
Animal Shelter
The End of Winter
Butterfly

All available from Amazon.co.uk and worldwide.

Poetry blog:
www.chatlyrique.blogspot.co.uk

Poetry Facebook Page:
www.facebook.com/LiteraryVegan/

Find out more about animal rights and veganism:

https://www.viva.org.uk/
https://www.vegansociety.com/
http://www.hsi.org/world/united_kingdom/
https://thehumaneleague.org/en_GB/

Thank you for reading.

Printed in Poland
by Amazon Fulfillment
Poland Sp. z o.o., Wrocław